T0153311

Winner of the IOWA POETRY PRIZE

Poems by Pamela Alexander

inland

University of Iowa Press Ψ Iowa City

University of Iowa Press,
Iowa City 52242
Copyright © 1997 by
Pamela Alexander
All rights reserved
Printed in the United States
of America

Design by Richard Hendel

http://www.uiowa.edu/~uipress

No part of this book may be
reproduced or used in any form
or by any means, electronic or
mechanical, including photocopying
and recording, without permission
in writing from the publisher. All
reasonable steps have been taken to
contact copyright holders of material
used in this book. The publisher
would be pleased to make suitable
arrangements with any whom it has
not been possible to reach. This is a
work of poetry; any resemblance to
actual events or persons is entirely
coincidental.

Printed on acid-free paper

Library of Congress Cataloging-in-Publication
Data

Alexander, Pamela, 1948–
   Inland: poems / by Pamela Alexander.
     p.   cm.–(Iowa poetry prize)
   ISBN 0-87745-582-1 (pbk.)
   I. Title. II. Series.
  PS3551.L3574I54 1997
  811'.54–dc21   96-51675
                            CIP

02 01 00 99 98 97 P 5 4 3 2 1

FOR MURIEL CORLISS ALEXANDER, 1904–1996

CONTENTS

ACKNOWLEDGMENTS

The author wishes to thank the editors of publications in which the following poems first appeared: *Agni:* "Manners"; *Atlantic:* "Accidentals," "Look Here"; *Beloit Poetry Journal:* "Origin"; *Chelsea:* "Lettered Olives," "Mt. Auburn Owl"; *Field:* "Fogbow," "Fortune," "Souvenir"; *Fire Readings: A Collection of Contemporary Writing from the Shakespeare & Company Fire Benefit Readings:* "Seminar"; *Lingo:* "Nots"; *New Republic:* "Mt. Pinatubo"; and *Prairie Schooner:* "What We Need."

Grateful acknowledgment is also extended to the MacDowell Colony and Ucross Foundation for residencies during which parts of this book were written.

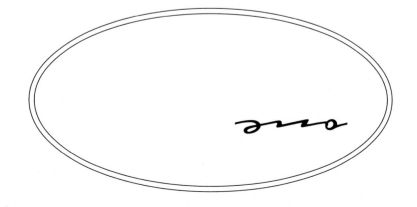

i

Things fell off shelves—hats, books, teakettles,
cats. My father among the ruins chanted
*Close the doors they're coming in the windows,
close the windows they're coming in the doors.*

Who were they? Would I recognize them?

The whole house fell down. *Row row row your boat*
—I saw a crow doing what my father sang,
stroke feather stroke—

as the crow flies. He knew when! Each beat!

Whoever, they were already inside
the house of him. His cottage industry: making
jokes, taking things literally. *Harvey Wallbanger
lives in Sheetrock. Window Rock's invisible,
Shiprock's another state altogether. Knock on wood,
you make a better door than window.*

ii

The mechanical bird stopped singing.
Then there was a war.

iii

The house grows up again, remembering.

The boy comes home with ideograms
in his lunchbox. Says it's important which direction
you make the strokes in, and in what order.

Later is not the same.

Church-mice have candlesticks. We're poor as bedbugs.
Halves, have nots. Afford a river? Never.
Row row row the boat I never thought
would float this far.

I have things. Coffee in the morning with a drop
of hazelnut. The boy's blue rocking-horse. Binoculars
to look at loons before they dive, books
about bridges. Trees in clay pots
and maps of many places.

                        The sea counts
but doesn't add. One
one   one   one   a series

of last times first middle all mixed up−

The boy counted two
and crowed.

Love's a hayride. A ladybug on your sleeve. Love's buggy! Love's horse.

Close the gates they're coming through the fences,
close the fields they're falling out of trees.

I am porch-sitting in cold air,
invigorated by coffee & first crocuses.
Bicycles tick.
Poodles with belled collars chink.
The mockingbird. Cats
that lived under the house all winter
uncrimp in my ivy beds. The pianist in the imitation
brick house
practices chords. Polyglot
starlings fold yellow feet around telephone wires
and drip onto the sidewalk. The doorbell rasps
at the funeral home across the street.
Awnings.
Major chords. A robin
whinnies. The truck with the state seal on its open door
shouts in its radio voice, Calling five. Five, do you copy?
Tax returns, the fat compliant envelopes,
thumped into mailboxes a few days ago. *The mockingbird.*
Showy tulips in the psychiatrist's garden
will open in a few weeks.
The bluejay doesn't jeer this time; its other call
drops two syllables, a stone into water.
What is the name of that spiky houseplant?
Soon it will sit on the porch more than I do, having the time.
Something to do with dragons. Minor
chords. Red edges. The escaped canary
sits in the maple all morning and doesn't make a sound.

Below the cliff, a sandless beach,
all smooth shards. Each footstep imagines
china can break slowly, and the incidental music
disconcerts an uneasy number of rats. They trot into weeds
too thin for cover, slip down tunnels that slant
into history: the island is artificial,
composed of a century's rubbish
brought here first under sail, then by barge
and stacked, a foot a year.

                                       What reconstruing
of the known, this matrix of bones and springs, of
ropes and spongy boards and
—up the clinking talus for a closer look—
yes, the lightest strata are newspaper
kept dry, perhaps, by the weight
of what came after. Tear a strip:
no date, an ad for soap.

                     Scuff
the littoral pottery. Poke through
tile and brick and the new arrivals, tires.
On the leeward shore (a smokestack, a few wrecked
buildings, some half-corroded drums)
the smell of burning garbage leaks
from inner, spontaneous fires.

The island's rectangular, a misplaced
mesa. From the channel it must look a delicate dessert,

layer pastry set on gleaming saucer, garnished
with a little greenery and too many egrets
—the occasional upflung wing or two
keeps them balanced.

Beaches breed regrets as well as rats (they hide
as quickly). The island's ugly, but the sun
—the sun comes out to touch it
with worthiness, however unlikely.
Those who have been around the place and leave
can see it again, all at once, stratum on stratum
of rust, taupe, rose, mustard, cobalt, literal bottle-green!
And tossed around the whole unaccountably elegant
mess, a scrappy scarf of beach, its colors worn and
worn out from the ocean's endless
one-liners, its all-night parties and repartee.

The white birds reflect last light
and fade. The wind rises. We didn't expect to hear
our island, but—
                    There. Again. As each wave falls
against the glazy rubble. Bells.

I lie on my back in the cemetery, elbows tight
to brace binoculars. He slides into focus
flat as bark, with bark's irregular thatchwork
of mothy grays and duns, his face kittenish
even to the cups of ersatz ears; he rises and falls
with my breathing.
                    And opens one
eye, camouflage undone by its depth
and expression (am I too human, finding malice
there?). Oak leaves fuss in our line of sight,
their gestures discomfited, Victorian,
all wrist and glove and rustling green dress
—too human indeed. I rise

from the horizontal others, walk in air flowing
with scents of blooming trees, the furtive silk of spring.

At the gate a thin man asks, See anything?
I tell him about the kingfisher by the pond,
its ratchety voice, about the water thrush
under the rhododendrons; slip
into the street, its heat and hurry.

Plunked on the dashboard all the way to Cape Breton
Island, beaky as toucans, those plump, white-breasted

sandbags of mine were not put off by my mother's misappellation
("going for a lark"), but by herself, above the Appalachians'

northern reaches — the pair, she said, would tempt a priest
to steal, and popped them in her handbag. And went for coffees

with two-thirds of the brood (Pemaquid long ago mailed to Manhattan,
with note: "Can we go out for sushi? Play in your bath-

tub? Oh goody!" leaving my mother the siblings, Pemaquid
and Pemaquid — no telling them apart), then unpursed, kissed,

re-dashed them, and sped with my father toward the real thing
— the big-footed, fish-gulping Atlantic Puffins on their nesting

grounds, or rather in their burrows — the rocky island all balconies
shining with tidy bellies, too many to count. Who could count? Only

those unaffected by *mal de mer* and by the captain's
hesitation at the chop thrown up by wind against tide. *Slam!*

— a wave the size of Moby Dick stranded on the open stern. Free-
board underwent a sea change. Fear cured nausea. Sluggishly,

Sea Jest II drained, wallowed into her turn, and bucked for home.
Puffins can keep Seal Island, or seals can, or the long gray boat-

buffeting bay itself, the captain said with his silence.

End of story? Almost.

Sated puffin-hunters puttered south to foggy Boston. Postscript:

I got my mother her own pack of jokers, her colony of potbellied
buffoons, of tubby, mime-faced tumblers. She named them Pemaquid

and Ptarmigan and Ptolemy, the last two no doubt after my late dog Pfoxer.
(My father demurred: "What about Pemigewasset? Passamaquoddy?"

and she said, "All right, then, we'll do murres next week, Eddie.")

(11

"Invent an animal," the teacher said.

"But," I cried, "I have stroked the guard hairs
of an armadillo. Isn't that enough?"

                             The teacher
paged back and forth. "Enough
is not an animal. Inhabit yourself widely."

"There are too many people for new animals,
too many even for known ones."

"The scales of a fish overlap
and fish overlap into schools. Unhand
yourself."

                       The field is vast
and gray, the grass cool beneath my paws.

They can flow uphill.

The largest reds live in Minnesota; the smallest
in Washington. Go to Kodiak Island for the bushiest
tail, Utah for the longest.

Day-sleeper,
not deeply. Works upwind
to choose a bed, circles,
settles facing downwind,

way-finder who will not show the way.

Way farer. Earns each day.
Duck eggs, in summer; ducks, whenever.
In the Horican marsh of Wisconsin,
Bradley Bowen shot a fox stalking decoys.

Cherries, grapes, blueberries. Acorns.
In the South, pecans. Autumn's crickets and grass-
hoppers, cold-stunned. Whole nests of yellow-jackets
dug up. Voles.

Late January: the vixen's
estrus. Scent stations mid-track for female,
to the side for male. Then

a double line of pawprints in the snow.

Dens are for pups. She leaves a few days
later, returning only to nurse. In six weeks
their eyes change from blue
to yellow; in October they'll pounce
on the first flake they see.

Soon they live
like adults, abroad, napping often, often on a rise,
less than a half a minute at a time, rested
by not-even-half-sleep, by
quarter-, sixteenth-sleep.

Foxlight, dusk-light, the kind she likes,
lets her pass unseen—undercover, low arrow
steadied by a brushy vane,

sleight-of-foot, sleight-of-fur, forest floor
slipper.

We are watched.

The house fell down on her, and cats
ran through the pieces—black
Aphrodite, tigers Ozymandias
and Electra, spawning tribes of kittens
in closets, bureau drawers, under
the mock-orange bush by the busy clothesline.
Beyond, in her wild garden,
the jacks, trilliums and lady-slippers
said it was spring, warbler weather—
wobbler, she said, native to the flyway
herself. (How many years since she'd picked up
and left Lake country, New Hampshire,
dropped south with her sisters? I wasn't
counting then; I wasn't.)
                                    The house tilted. Things slid
and spilled. Gangs and generations and leagues of things.

One shelf held. Housed
her fountain pen, thick and imperial,
and the opera glasses with which she followed the careers
of nuthatches, hawks and gaudy jays. All else
worn out, broke down, lost at sea.

Her nibs.
Her outlook.

Of a line of quiet folk: her mother sat with the Bible;
her father with his cold pipe stared at the fire;
Great Aunt Grace, Great Uncle Enoch, old in Laconia

all my life, she of the violin voice and rocker, he
silent as the deer head his gun got.

She read late
under cats, beside cats, the dishes stacked cockeyed,
Aphie crouched on the counter
lapping at the top saucer—Rachel Carson
and Edwin Way Teale and Dorothy Sayers
and Will Durant, dog-eared. She read late because things fell
into place: all of us asleep, him at work,
her in bed with coffee and archeology.
Mesopotamian nights! She read to place herself,
a light on until he came home.

The mansion is full of spiders. Pick up
a large one — it stands in your palm and weighs
some amount muscles recognize. Less
than a lemon. More than a letter. The smallest
look like dust, but when you blow them
off the mantel they don't fall far (dust
can't save itself). The spiders slide
up and down, measuring tall windows for drapes
and then sketching them in.
The village is hours away but the land flat,
so that matins and vespers reach our inner ears.
Studying the intersection of attachment
and freedom, the spiders tremble like the hands of
Trappists — not from the work of the heart
(a spider's is unchambered) but of the spinneret,
which fibrillates, beams out
viscous geometries.
                         On the landing,
in its tub the size of a baby grand,
the philodendron stirs. It taps woody rhizomes
against the treads going downstairs,
the risers going up. The spiders
take in light and give off, at night,
a high and wiry hum. You will hear it
soon. The only rule is you must
walk from room to room, floor to floor.
You must not lie down on the parquet.
The mansion has many flights; we will not see
each other again. The only rule is you must not
touch anything. You must not sing back.

MANNERS

Sit, she said. The wolf sat. Shake, she said.
He held his face and tail still
and shook everything in between. His fur
stood out in all directions. Sparks flew.
Dear sister, she wrote. His yellow eyes
followed the words discreetly. I have imagined
a wolf. He smells bad. He pants, and his long tongue
drips onto the rug, my favorite rug. It has arrows
and urns and diamonds in it. The wolf sits
where I've stared all morning hoping
for a heron: statuesque, aloof,
enigmatic. Be that way, the wolf said.
There are other poets.

Normal rowing's an exercise
in hindsight—you face astern, toss glances
over a shoulder to judge progress. I rowed
backwards, the blunt orange bow ahead.
I nudged it against the flow, at a certain
angle to the bank of Georgian mud
and marsh grass, allowing ten feet or so of shallows
—swarming, we hoped, with shrimp. He gathered
the net and hung it on the air. It opened
and dropped, crooked. He cast again.

My part was slight, given
the inflatable's scant draft and the habit
of breeze to lie down for a nap
near sunset. I made ellipses with my fistfuls of oar
that the oars, in their bladed way,
translated into leverage: the dinghy
stood. Its pontoons sagged a little
as the air inside them cooled; his footing
softened. He cast a dozen times,
a score. Weights the size of larch cones
(they sounded larger) fringed the net;
each time he gathered it to coherence
they met in a leaded *thook* with a hint
of ring, like pewter mugs bumped in salute.

But not by us. He was fixed
on the net, on making it fall
a perfect circle—as if that would draw

shrimp, or luck, or whatever
he was after. Behind us a dolphin sighed
and no doubt showed its dark fin; I watched
his back and he watched the net's
arc and splash. And when the light drained
to a corner of sky, he must have thrown
by heft and angle and heart, needing the dim print
amid watery stars—his speech, his chart.

Drain
doesn't; pump
won't. Policeman
shot the possum, didn't
know what else to do.
Couldn't feel the hands
pulling at his coatsleeve? The boy had
who'd found the thing
and brought it home to Mum.

Point
No Point, south
of Newport News. Named
for its obscurity: even Noah wouldn't
see it, a man who thirsted so
for land. (Noah was a raven too,
rode my shoulder, shot by decree
when he tried his one best trick
on a stranger dressed like me.)

We begin, we end. In between,
facts & feelings box the compass.
Some inescapable motion's got us, prompts our
comings & goings, the jostling of molecules
magnified.
It's more noticeable when there's no explanation for it,
nothing but necessity, too simple
for reasons. The kind of accident
that isn't.

The board game Go developed in China
where nobody plays it anymore;
it's popular in Japan. The object,
to surround territory
using black & white stones
as markers. Patterns emerge.
Beyond that, the game resists explanation.

I didn't mean to be going anywhere.
What I don't mean
happens anyway. Surrendering territory
is unavoidable; a life, the longest distance
between two points.
The compass rose blooms everywhere.

Maps make good pets, constant and friendly.
When I get someplace I look it up,
can't find it anywhere.
I can go only as far

as I will never come back from.
You will never.
This is not a voluntary arrangement.

Sooner or later everything darkens.
The dusting of pastels in spring woods,
for instance; or foghorns
in the harbor, two different pitches
at different intervals
repeating so often I didn't hear them
and their accidental harmonies
until I'd left town.

The difference between here and there
is sometimes important. Meanwhile, the mind
wanders off course. The mind makes itself up.

We look at each other
in the plum-colored dusk.
Does it have to be so late?
People are walking, and in the dim light
I can't tell if they are moving closer
or farther away.

The magician's trunk in the garage
belonged to my grandfather, him
of the horsehair chair that scratched,
Professor Sherbert and a house painter.
After he died we discovered
there was nothing in it.

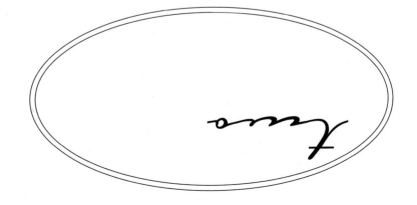

Morning, we think:
a glow, and the cratcheting of a few birds,
or frogs, an hour back. On deck the light's brighter
but still diffuse, and damp, and featureless.
Current splits around the hull in ripples
that convince us we're under way
but for some unfamiliar sense, a nudge in the brain
we take to mean *holding*. The mast-top
dissolves; the anchor line runs out taut
and ends in diffidence, pinning us to nothing
but space made visible, all gray foreground
unwilling to admit a thing.

Against the white, a whiter arc
touches its ends to what must be
its own reflection: to starboard, where
the sky usually loiters, cloud-close or infinite,
an oval hovers. I kneel on wet teak to watch
the concoction of light and obscurity—my first
fogbow, new category of illusion.

CQR
       (obscure
Brit. pun): plow-type, good
for all holding ground except weed
(kelpy pods & ribbons in which nothing sets)
and drifts of bottles & alum. cans, shiftiest,
found below popular
watering holes. Sea-cu-re.
Sold the boat, sloop, suit of 7 sails
from spinnaker to (bikini) storm jib, selling her whole-
sale, keel to antenna tip, with fenders & lines & inflatable
dinghy. & sense organs (boatish ones): knotmeter paddle
tips pro-
truding, just, into
slipstream, & anemometer
scoops, sky-backed & squinted at, blurred
with speed (but repeater bulkhead-mounted, eye-kind). Paradoxical voice,
ultrasoprano aimed low, sounding depth on 2 scales, feet/fathoms. More:
two-lung
primitive engine,
rated at 12 (sea) horses, puny
by land standards but *deus ex machina* in flat sun-
sets (boom slatting, sails slumped & wrinkled, forgetting
the shapes that translate speed to speed). Goddish bounteous windy
wandering! Sold her, fiberglass,
dacron, sad.
Because you were unhappy
with me, out there. Sold myself the story
of the oar & baker's peal, of going so far lifelines are social,

orange vests worn by traffic cops & mastheads two-dimensional.
You were
(that's right, wave)
never (bye bye) at home at sea. Too impatient to be windborne.
Sold the lot, at a loss (my slicker turned city-), cashed in hully home
to be inlander, glassy cliff dweller, bank swallow in elevators. Keepsake:
the anchor, for its shape {25 lbs. of rough galvanized sheer
bifurcated, two wings arcing away from each (NW) (NE),
but joined & braced}, and for its intent:
to hold come hell

Ashfall,
        bluish.
Cabins deranged, edging forward.
Guardrails hot! Highway incoherent,
jack-knifed.
        Luminous
midnights. Noonday owls, plumages quivering.

Rivers steam. Trees take umbrage,
undressed.

        Violence waits, waits. Exhales, waits.
Explodes: year zero.

Foursquare & seven years ago
met him, followed, lived
together, had in common
cats, dog, house, bed: now forswear
all—animals dead, house sold,
furniture Mayflowered to his new city,
his proving ground.
Here winter clicks the earth shut
and my front door, fresh-painted,
shudders when it opens: force wears
such ordinary clothing. Each dawn labors
to build what evening will foreclose,
a small lit place amid the dark. Seven
years. The heart winces
at its own history. And mythology,
that imaginary past, is no better:
Cupid's fat forebodes cardiac
delusion, a terminal condition. Hear him
tinkering in the chandelier; consider
the relative sizes of the human heart and his
spears. Oh forbear. No man's created equal,
nor woman, to all this foregoing.

Next time you walk by my place
in your bearcoat and mooseboots,
your hair all sticks and leaves
like an osprey's nest on a piling,
the next time you walk across my shadow
with those swamp-stumping galoshes
below that grizzly coat and your own whiskers
that look rumpled as if something's
been in them already this morning
mussing and growling and kissing,
the next time you pole the raft of you downriver
down River Street past my place
you could say *hello*, you canoe-footed fur-faced
musk ox, pockets full of cheese and acorns
and live fish and four-headed winds and sky, *hello*
is what human beings say when they meet each other
—if you can't say hello like a human don't
come down this street again and when you do don't
bring that she-bear and if you do I'll know
even if I'm not on the steps putting my shadow
down like a welcome mat, I'll know.

1

A door can be nothing
but dramatic. Openings! Exits! Nevertheless,
two stone steps underline the cabin door.

Inside, sun lies across the piano. Slides
onto the bench, touches the keys—January
sunlight, too weak to play.

2

The cabin sits squarely
as a chair. Considers the inspirations
of footstalks, branchiness: the forest's
provisions for getting leaves in the way of light.

Heart's-ease, bloodroot, you have gone underground.

The ladders of reason can go as far
as they have something to lean against.

Sunlight falls down. Then it gets up
in the shape of trees.

Chickadees percolate through hemlock, tamarack
—punctuation, loosed and ranging.

A trail can only be narrative.

3

The new year crossed my path in the form of a fox
bristling with snow. Mice on her mind. She jumped
at a few, missed. Dry flakes ticked among the grasses.
Beneath her red hairs, gray underfur.

The fox leaves tracks like asterisks.

I make conversation, arranging
two strips of bacon on a rock.
Which sign will call the fox? An X, a plus?
a sign for intersection? for equal?

4

Midnight. Windy. A trailside bush
flashes, bright. I wade in, mitten a branch still,
and find a chip of frost, dime-sized,
making change for moonlight.

Trees click their sugar-sticks against each other.
Quiet, please! I am following a reticence, a fast-
fur, pheasant-sacker, blood-biter.

5

Hunger.

Do not lean the ladders of reason
against a burning house.

Wit's end. What starts here
is another element.

I make myself a sentence good enough to eat.

Moon through fog. At eye level, a dissonance of gray
among grays. Then a scramble:
a band of boiling white lengthens.
Falls, fades.
        Breakers. The world set at such an angle
that only the hurried signature shows
of the whole, the boisterous, wave.
            Befogged. My knees feel
the slope toward the waves, slight. The sand firms and cools
toward the watery scree, toward the invisible rush
that dissipates with a hiss.

A different light, a widening, a color
inventing color. The sand glows blue, orange,
gold. Sprawled plants in the dunes
reveal red in their leaves, which are lightly furred,
veined. Dry black birds with crooked necks
creak overhead. *Oh what? What for?*

1

Right ear higher than left, thus
stereo hearing, like ours, but locating
more precisely on the vertical axis. Scanning—

The opening eight times ours. Hears
mouse tooth chip seed,
vole tail touch bark,
leaf land. Hears even
herons haul up their long legs
and trail them south.
Stays.

Stays by us. Calls in the dark,
through the dark, searching.
Smells oil in the night breeze,
the gritty bite of gear teeth. Clicks
its beak. Flies deeper. Calls out

—not to us. But we go,
we owl followers. We open
the night air and, groundlings,
shiver awake in a stand of pine.

Great Horned, Barn, Screech. Dead-of-winter
breeders. They stir the dark like distant dogs
but are not distant.
O we are surrounded.

2

Twigs swell. Warm air crosses the sill.
Soil loosens, releasing its leaf-bitten,
stone-colored smell.

What axis do we
live on? Not time, which bends,
is sharped and flatted, has keys. What
locate, call out to, after knowing
this year, that year, the thing that includes both?

Early clematis: purple cones displace
last year's pinwheel husks.
Petals open flat as books; the wind browses

and brings their scent to the bed
mixed with metallic sear of window screens.

Sweat. Just a sheet, as at the end.
Be afraid. Be careful
to be afraid of worthy things.

3

Clematis! Clitoris! Listen, this *is*
our body, earth, clutter of rock, mist,

rough road lit on one side, late
light. The bushes flicker
with small birds. Late.

Are there still wolves?

How long have we been here?

A minute. A minute. The wind.

Just inside the gate, two rabbits
ran from us in that unsuccessful manner
they have sometimes, ahead, choosing
the same direction we planned: the path between
the spy ponds. At last they hid.
We walked the ridge that lifted us
along vast draperies of spruce. Silent.
Then the loop back into the open, to find
great-crested flycatchers, flaring and settling, high.
We'd watched the flamboyant pair
flaunting their crests and rufous tails
for ten minutes before I recognized
the owl-oak. Lowered the binoculars from the crown,
found the knot-hole. Found the bark-gray one
and—more than I knew to wish for—next to him,
larger, shyer, cinnamon and gold, his mate, who
retreated at my call to you, my slip: Two. There are two of us!

Of the family of weasels, European polecats & ferrets,
but better-humored: the most playful wild creature, devoting
whole afternoons to climbing muddy banks & coasting down
(the slide improves with use); and nosing turtles
back & forth like frisbees; and bumping, underwater;
and chasing one another about the watercourse,
flexing long brown bodies in cursive loops,

> the message clear. We

second it — no, we third and fourth it. Whiskered
like a river otter, you, and as slender.
There's a name for what we make. Let's
not say it, let's float on it a while
the way our furry cousins, surfaced, rest,
eyes & nose & whiskers up, let's hold here,

> blanket to our chins, & drift.

SPILL

It's October; we left the ferns on the back porch one night too many; now we have fern-shape and even fern-color but no ferns. The woman who lived here before us kept losing her canaries — not eyeglasses or car keys, but canaries; of course they do move by themselves which is more than you can say for the average pair of glasses, but on the other hand you can't see a canary better with another canary. She must have had a theory, though; she got a second bird, and lost it, and then another; she told us this by way of warning, if we should find them. We never did, but then we had a cat, two cats, Scotch and Soda, until Soda ran away or did we lose her?

So it's October and we light a fire with twists of paper; our friend has the proper term for them — "spills" — the same friend who told us about the kind of desert rat that never drinks, never, and about *linea alba*, the white seam down the front of all of us; think of that, those muscles have to attach somewhere and it's in the middle, an axis of lightness in each of us. The phrase makes me think of dawn even though dawn doesn't happen in the middle of anything but at the beginning or the end. All this time we thought we were adrift we had a line in the middle like roads; how could we have lost our way? There's nothing better than a fire in the early cold, we all feel renewed, ready for difficult things; maybe I will ask our friend about relativity after all. What's the opposite of an aubade? We won't get up early enough for one, but we have the weekend to eat ice cream in bed together as a way of celebrating cold and warmth at the same time. Still mostly under the blankets, we'll lean out the window, wishing the ferns weren't dead and the basil and impatiens hadn't frozen, a cold snap everyone calls it, which sounds too human, like bones. We'll lean our bones into the weather, feel the ache of the sill across our stomachs and the muscles working to keep us here. Of course we knew about the white line, we just misplaced its name for a number of years. It's hard to see things when you are them. We found a couple of feathers.

Up the dim hemlocked trail, we passed
glacial erratics big as houses and brightened
by tapestries of lichen and moss.
Pondside, I dropped my pack and sat, still
as the water.
                    Flat calm. No fish broke
its surface, no algae colored it,

leeches didn't decorate its
shallows with swimming ribbons, pastel
green above and red below. No twig broke
in the summer woods around us; even the light,
tangled in some bright trap, was still.

Another erratic! A sandpiper I'd somehow missed
until it bobbed, mid-pond, three times. After that it
looked huge, on its mud-bar, unmissable, still
or not. A least 'piper, typically coastal—they'll pass
in flocks just overhead, changing the light
when they bank as one: breakers above breakers.

Did this bird prime some pump when it broke
the quiet? Footsteps squelched through moss
and you came out of swamp brush into full light
along a half-sunk log so broad it
looked flat—two people could pass
each other on that bleached roadway and still

have space between. I followed you.
                              Stillness
magnified everything: the checkered bark, breaking
evenly as masonry when mortar fails; past
the log's base, a forest—reddish sphagnum moss
and hundreds of roseate sundew. On its
dense fur, sweet viscid globes snared the light.

Bouquets of pitcher plants glowed, veins highlighted
maroon: vegetable animals, carnivorously still.
—We looked at the sterile, acidic pond, admired its
richness and spareness. And turned away.
                              Breaking
bark and ferns underfoot, you caught a mosquito
for me to feed to sundew jaws; it pulled free as you passed

it. A slight creature, slightly broken
but still flying.
                 And we still meet and miss,
finding passion feeds a luminous impasse.

UNDERSTORY

i

The hay scented. The cinnamon, the horsetail,
the interrupted; maiden-hair, royal, ostrich, marsh!
The sensitive. The walking. The
resurrection! Ferns.

ii

In the big claw-footed tub,
washing each other for the first time.
You said, Don't let me forget
it can be like this.

iii

We looked down for a minute, at most.
What was it? Some wildflower
or moss, or one of those fluorescent orange newts
we'd startled with every step. When I stood up
a spider's web glistened
between the straps of your binoculars.
How long have we been here?

No boat safe without anchor, cipher for earth,
pinned to the bow,

sculpted like a stocky bird
and trained to dive for a living (ours). Chain rackets
after it, chased by the quiet line, the rode. Watch
the markers blur over the side as we pay out 25 feet, 50, 100 −

The boat falls back slowly, just
a notch, from the long day's push. No
bubbling under the transom now, and without the breeze
the sun stings our necks and arms. Watch

and when you see the rode consider straightening,
snub it to the big cleat. We're ashore,

so to speak, the flukes resting on mud
down there, or rock − we're not done, not
sure we've struck the ore
of good holding ground

and stuck. So: find features
ashore, one to each side. Steeple, yes. Pier.
Sight rough bearings, wear them like a big windy
shirt with long sleeves.

The bow nods to starboard, hangs,
returns, magnetic needle wavering

above a recently discovered
pole—as still as we can be

and be with wind on water. The rode
is almost humming. Can the bird sing
from her deep nest? Listen:

the sweet line creaks in its chock.
Droplets stand out from the triple braid, expressed
by strain. Wait.

Steeple still abeam? Pier above the first
stanchion? Good. We're down. We're tight. We've used
the weight of boat to dig us in. What's the depth
here? Add six for tide. Let out three times the sum
in feet of rode. That number

—no matter what's out there, fish-scaled
palm trunks, say, with pelicans
lumbering over, or terns and pine trees
making finer distinctions—no matter
what, that number's our home town, our address.

We came dazzled
from the beach, pockets pouched with shells —
conchs and orange scallops
and three prizes we would later name,
from the guidebook, lettered olives.
It was cool under the live oaks, the branches
hung with moss like delicate laundry
always too damp to take in.
The droppings of wild horses stood up
in cairns, prominent as buoys but marking no
clear channel. We picked different routes
toward the columned, double-staircased front,
the once-Vanderbilt "cottage" that grew
into a compendium of disrepair:
windows glassless, stairs crumbling, roof
a sundeck for weeds, porch planks warped and cranky.
We trusted the porch swings and sat
and grounded with a slam that scared us and scared loose
a cat to distract us from our mishap (did the chains, fat as the one
our boat swung by, stretch?). The cat was friendly,
black with white bib and whiskers, glossy,
well-kept — here, where we had opened ourselves
to the beauty of abandonment.
He followed us full circuit as we peered
into tall rooms indistinguishable
for their emptiness and dust; he leaned expertly
against our legs, trying each of us in turns — a purring
puzzle, a house cat not of this house

nor was there another on the island. Yet he stopped
just beyond the weedy drive and paced
a boundary, back and forth,
and did not follow to the beach.

Remind me. Was it just our tiredness? Or were things askew?
Beyond the ocotillo and prickly pear, far out in the speckled dunes,

a rainbow groped for its footing — one end diffuse, the other tangled
in a water tank's braced aluminum legs. Nothing was settled

— not the rainbow, not the wickery basket some tumbleweeds
began to build in a wire fence corner, and began again, re-

grouping as we passed. Not even the towns looked fixed;
was Red Mesa this grove of shacks, or that? And did

Mexican Water move in the wind? We saw smaller, dirt-tracked,
two-truck places, one beside a dry wash where a coyote panted,

stick-ribbed, lying flat, lifting only her head toward our engine.
Flies scribbled the air around her eyes. Oh, if

water were not withheld, saved up in cloud-banks —

Remind me (but you can't). How was it we'd come that way?
under a river of blue light, nimbus stacked on either side and frayed

where rain tugged it down, then vanished. Our first desert
(you never traveled) and rain any minute, we said,

as the atmospheric trick cleared us a roadway in the clouds.
(Wrong place, I said, this car flies low. I wish I'd understood.)

One downpour swayed its smoky column on the horizon; the rest
of the great space stayed dry as a snake. The road essed into a forest

of saguaro, sparse and pale, mixed with the stylized towers
strung with high-voltage lines. You said how dark it was.

The day turned on its blazing hub; our earthbound wheels
put up a commotion of dust into which disappeared

a struggling bicyclist, dust-colored himself, headed nowhere
near. I knew *his* future, at least: hills, and the mountain where,

the night before, snow whispered against our windshield.

                           −No, the landscape
is not what I wish to change. Even if we had shaken the rain

from its shelves and stuck the rainbow into sand
firmly as a wicket, we would have left the place just the same

and gone to where we had to go. I suppose it was your
business to die. I wish you'd let me revise a detail or two

or several, or all. You had other business, too.

& cannot end, not, at least, in the way

hereinafter called the party of the first, etc.,

underfoot

a butterfly of the genus *Polygonia*, having brownish,
irregularly notched wings

graphical shrimp

The forest understory consists of bramble, habitat for hares.

somersault, backwards

pseudopod

depression between the muzzle and top of the skull
of a dog

tripwire, snare for rabbits

, that one cannot begin to

Housepainters deploy themselves against
my sleep; no dream can bear the super-
impositions of ladders

                         –screechers, wallbangers,
blizzards of aluminum rattlery. A house can stand
to be without such clamberousness, to hang in the wind
minus crutches, its own foursquare-
ishness sufficing. A house can stand for a great deal,
holding its ends up in rainscrim, ice, in shimmery heat.
A house can sleep.

                    Yesterday, giddy
with death, I discovered *real* in *real estate*
means *material*. Imbedded in woodframe
and slumber, sipping my breaths
from the fogged waterglass of pre-August
August heat, I wake to my unwariness.
The world's reality is solid; things
press against each other and continue un-
interrupted. Something in us does not. I object
to death in general and one, recently
accomplished, in particular.

                         The clapboards shriek
under the scrapers' blades. What's
a life? A warmth, indwelling, easily dispersed
(even though the body, that material
witness, lies, *present*); an unreliable vapor, white

camisole under the ordinary mayhem of making do, slip,
slipped away. I pronounce death
realer than real estate, louder than ladders,
and I bang my head against it and shake.

You were not there, in the Sonoran.

I drove you through towns near your house—
Dover and Sherborn and the ones
that begin with M. We got lost together.

Now an old man walks down the middle of the road.

Not there. I wrote you in
because I left you.

He looks at each house carefully
as if he has never seen it before.

Back from the desert, I found you wearing
a headstone too new to have its second date.

Dirt in his hair. He lives at the end of the road.
He walks slowly and talks to himself.

Here you are: trillium by the porch,
Japanese fern, leaky gutter, chickadees, ants
in the kitchen, bookmark
in the encyclopedia at "piano."

He comes every Saturday to sell flowers,

rings the bell and calls me by your name.
He smiles, glad to see you 40 years younger.

Here. I sleep with the doors wide open
but you don't leave.

1 Ipswich

We drift around the bend, silent, paddles over gunwales.
On either side a scrimmage of cardinal flower, marsh
marigold, poisonous Indian poke

from which we must look
like a short-winged dragonfly.

        Astern, I dig into black water. The stroke
stirs an eddy—tiny inverse of tornado, dry funnel into wet—
that draws a spiral in the floating pollen. But my eye
catches a different spinning on
the bank ahead, an emptiness just as
I look—a circular nothing, tinged with rust,
and a single branch nodding
to no breeze—
Fox. Must have been.

2 Plum Island

Young, coat still downy
—and incautious, to walk into a road, even
such a slow, rutted, dirt one, and to turn toward
the car, even engine-cut, coasting, stopped.

States her sex
and perhaps her opinion of road

with its odors of oil and exhaust
by squatting, signing it with her dark puddle.
Sniffs the air in our direction and ambles
into brown grass, disappearing before she's gone.

3 Punta Blanca

In matter's smallest
matters, we can't know both
what and *where* at the same time; *so*

what? is half the story; so

what stalks my mind is not
the nonchalant vixen openly pissing
but the fox I didn't see, turning
me with his stronger valence, the power of
the almost-seen, the almost-absent. I

want the fox.
But more I want that
place he goes, behind the light.

Late. What light's left, curious too, leans over my shoulder
as I shove the door open. Edges past me
into the barn I've found on a bad road

halfway down this small mountain.

I'm ungulate in stiff boots, earthbound Aries
on the loose. Slow talker. Fox tracker. Multiple names
for one life. *Not one; looks like one.*

Smell of sawdust. Familiar shape—
someone's rebuilding a boat. Odd place for a boathouse.
She's just 20 or 22 feet, on jackstands,
bottom paint dull blue nearby,
gray beyond the reach of door-glow.

You've been here before. No. Yes.
The boat I owned; other people's boats
I've worked on, boats in cradles
boarded by ladder and
drilled, hammered, caulked, wired. Aboard
Moonshadow, 32 feet of home to my friends: shears
grinding through glass cloth, fibers
floating in the cabin's air, sharp smell
of the resin that hardened the glistening stuff in place.
Chalk-blue paint on my hands.
Varnish. And that ark

Archetype, high in a field, in Hamilton. Belonged to
someone I didn't know—but she was mine, too,
because of the work I gave. *That's how one is more.*

This little one unnamed, half-decked. Topsides fresh-cut, shining
in the gloom. Deck joists curved so finely they look flat,
some with pencilled notes, indecipherable
in this light, soon to be planked over,
worked through waves with all the rest.

You left the boats,
your boat. Wasa, a Swedish name
awash in puns. Was a wave tripper,
wind walker. Was a place to stand.

Fifteen years since I crewed to Nova Scotia,
got rowed ashore from Moonshadow.
Up beach, field, slapface through woods
toward a road sketched on the chart's edge.
Sand-pounder, pack-bearer,
mule. Map for chart, boots for sails. Dirt-walker.
Hitched a ride on a schoolbus playing hooky,
a couple with three daughters "goin' to see the States."
Canoe lashed to the roof; bicycles racked
astern, their wheels dabbling in the slipstream—
paddlewheeler, bus-house.
Namer. You have names for the child
you never had.

I follow the bad road to the top, its view
of the corrugated ocean
and of clouds dragging long shadows beneath them
like trawlers' nets. Below me the road floods
twice a day; the note in my pocket, directions here,
reads "Wait."

The water's always brighter than the land.

And wilder. Yes, wilderness. *Had your own
boat. Sold it.* But the first sail was quiet,
under jib only, finicky sunset breeze.
I flicked the sheet along the deck
like a farmer slapping reins
on the rumps of his team, except
I had all the horsepower of the ocean (well, the harbor)

and she obeyed! Bow bluffed its way
through wavelets that shivered at the waterline;
dusk-light, small water-talk; the island rocked
ahead, large, larger, dark
Misery Island. Great Misery. Two coves, both often
empty, then. Years ago. That night big Moonshadow
waiting, anchor-light aloft.

I dropped the awkward fluky thing
off the bow, let out scope, waited. And they laughed
at how far out I was, novice, shore-shy—

Was a life you could have had.

Black vultures cut through, heading
inland: enough light for their last pass
over the salt marsh. Later this summer they'll see
the little boat with stowed words
launched from ledge below birches
or following the ebb out
through marshgrass—land-made, sea-led
to the ancient whale-paths, the deep places.

Like those two aboard Moonshadow,
land-met, sea-wed.

        Foghorn and thunder; an evening squall
works its way downwind. Plane
drone. Foghoot.
        Silence,

two or three
        acres of it.

A dream woke me: Yelling into the phone,
Don't take the check, Jay, tell them I've changed my mind,
I'm keeping her. *You would have been calling from Iowa,*
surrounded by cornfields and horse barns
and Amish who wouldn't look at you, you outlander, you
English—and a woman, alone, a freak, for pity.

The sky and sea confer
about the night's degree of darkness.

Late.

Make the best of the half-light you live in—
Your course never straight, wobble-wake
maker, boat or not, fishing for answers
with too wide a net. The child I couldn't decide on
won't wake me crying loud as grief, won't answer
her name called toward the long dusk.

One can be lived as more than.

But my branch of the family tree
ends here. What to do but cut it, plane it,
shape a boat, raise a sail?

The wind blows a moon up, stirs
the pines with their wooden flowers.
Small mountain
like a land wave.

Foghorn. Dreamspin.
Boathouse scraps assemble
to cradle a boat of air. Negative boat,
the most open. Stars for running lights.
I stand in it and sing hard, the waves
high as I can imagine.

HOUSE SONG

One may delight in one's house, a body
after all. Made of beams! joi-
sts! May accept just this
somatic attitude, this bearing
on true north, angle of sunlight
mitred against the floor. Flute
at dawn, oboe at noon. Openness
contained, like a book—walls
of books, and the switchback road, reading,
that traverses steep cuts of print:
back and forth the mind
conducts itself

            (a motion
I recognize, held me once, ocean-wise)

—a house is an upside boat
down. Slides through currents
with rooftree keel; starfish stars
swim under. Leaves a wake,
phosphorescent Milky Way. Lapstrake
clapboards, courses of them, deflect spray.
Mast? The long shadow cast up
through dirt, and aquifer, and ledge,
through time's geological atmospheres,
toward the center fixed and fluid. Home.

A roof over
three squares.
Warmth to wear,
something to burn

in winter. Water
music: sheets
of rain hung out
to dry. Time, or

the habits of light.
A road that thins
in hills. Hills.
Once an image

sufficed; now I see
we must speak.